My mother was such a good role model. She taught me by example to be kind-hearted, considerate and a loyal friend.

Mother Knows Best

Mother Knows Best

precious words of wisdom from mothers
to their children

RYLAND PETERS & SMALL
LONDON • NEW YORK

Senior designer Toni Kay
Picture research Christina Borsi
Production controller Meskerem Berhane
Art director Leslie Harrington
Editorial director Julia Charles
Publisher Cindy Richards

First published in 2015 by
Ryland Peters & Small
20–21 Jockey's Fields
London WC1R 4BW
and
341 E 116th St
New York
NY 10029

www.rylandpeters.com

ISBN 978-1-84975-615-0

A CIP record for this book is available
from the British Library.

US Library of Congress CIP data
has been applied for.

Printed and bound in China.

Contents

Introduction

Mothers pass on so much more than mere genes to their children. They shape us in myriad ways, many of which we don't really appreciate until we are fully grown and perhaps have our own children. Often we unconsciously echo our mothers in our gestures, phrases, and even the way we laugh or walk, and we find ourselves remembering her philosophical words in times of adversity.

This book is a reflection of that shared experience. Although many of the words here belong to individuals, they contain much useful advice and insight on finding one's way in the world, overcoming doubt or disappointment, and making the most of the good times, too.

From treasured childhood memories to the times when she gave you love, comfort, security and understanding when it was most needed, to the words of wisdom she blessed you with and that you have carried with you into adulthood as her legacy, this book says a heartfelt thank you to one of the most special people in your life – your mother.

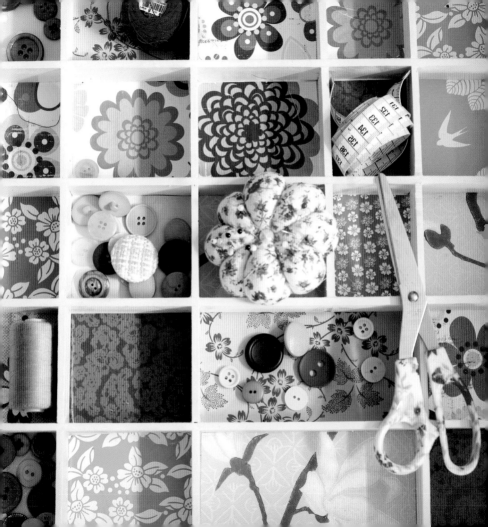

Love

Love sought is good,
but giv'n unsought is better.

William Shakespeare

"As a grown woman, having truly grounded and centered myself within who I am in this world, I feel I am finally able to give back to my mother on a deeper level than I recognized was possible when I was younger. We are sisters, friends, mother and daughter and soul mates."

"A mother's love is a
remarkable thing."

"Add a pinch of love to everything that you do. It makes life taste sweeter."

"When I was little, my mother did all sorts of crafty things. She sewed most of my clothes, my dance costumes, and all my fancy Easter dresses. Though she never claimed to be a great cook, nobody could make Chili con Carne like her. She seemed chronically busy, her work never done, yet she managed plenty of affection for me when I needed it, and never complained when I followed her around and bothered her. Looking back, I took it all for granted. I recognize now that although we had our arguments, she always managed to love me unconditionally. She showed by example that love was at the top and bottom of everything. Somehow she knew I'd figure things out in time. She was right."

"It's important to love yourself and treat yourself as well as you treat other people. Pay attention to your appearance, because if you feel good on the outside, it will help you feel good on the inside."

"Years ago my heart was broken when the friend I had fallen in love with didn't feel the same. My mother counselled me to keep the friendship and see how my own feelings changed over time. Now the friend is married, and I count her and her husband amongst my closest friends and enjoy happy times with them and their son, who is my godchild."

"As a daughter you have the fortune to be cared for by your mother; the question is, do you have the intelligence to appreciate her? We each love, fight, learn and grow from each other. I had the luck to appreciate my mother before she passed away – before her time – and the luck of having four amazing children of my own. I am one of the lucky ones. Tell your mother now how much you appreciate her, and tell your own children how much they are worth!"

And ever has it been
known that love knows not
its own depth until the time
of separation

Kahlil Gibran

"My mother taught me to be generous in matters of the heart, even when the love is coming to an end. I had already bought some (expensive) concert tickets for both of us when my boyfriend and I broke up. She advised me to treat the night out as his redundancy pay! I learned that it's best to part amicably, if you can."

"The relationship I have with my mother is one of love, and a knowing that she's always there for me if I need her. I don't live at home and we're both busy with our own lives, so we don't get the opportunity to meet up very often. However, we never let a day go by without texting each other, asking how the day went, and telling one another how much we love each other."

Love without conditions, and encourage
your child's dreams.

Security

A mother is a mother still,
The holiest thing alive.

Samuel Taylor Coleridge

"I enjoy a wonderful relationship with my children. Our bond is based on our desire to provide each other with an emotionally safe place that we can always depend on, no matter what happens in our own lives."

"My mother accepts the worst things about me and still loves me in spite of my flaws and idiosyncrasies. She is always there with a box of tissues or a much-needed cooked dinner. After all, there is nothing like a mum to comfort you, whether it is with food or just love."

20 Security

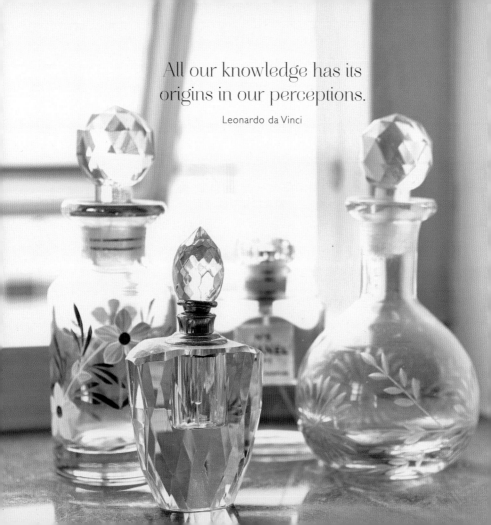

All our knowledge has its origins in our perceptions.

Leonardo da Vinci

"The minute my first child was born, I was flooded with a new sensation, a yearning to protect and hold close. It was as if a strong, territorial force compelled me to stay nearby – and I was shocked by the emergence of a love so profound that I could scarcely describe it. Though everything about having a baby and being a mother was new to me, I recognized my part intuitively, and felt a primal bond. I took him to my breast, my eyes fixed on his small face, and I became an instant authority on all things concerning him."

"My mother is my rock. She taught me how to face adversity, rise above it and come out stronger. A single mother, she moved across the country to give us a fresh start. She has always been a symbol of love and strength for me. If it wasn't for her wisdom and guidance, I wouldn't be the person I am today. Every day, I wake up wishing I could give her the life she always dreamed of. The one thing I can always give her is my love."

Nothing can bring a real sense of security into the home except true love.

"As a toddler, my daughter became enthralled with the scent of my perfume, the aroma of the fabric softener I used in our laundry and, well, just the regular smell of me. Whenever we went out into public places, she'd bury her face in my skirt, and breathe deeply. I didn't realize it at the time, but my daughter was insecure and frightened, and my smell made her feel secure and safe when she wasn't feeling much of either. I had recently remarried, and travelled regularly for my job, which meant that she and her sister often had to stay behind with a babysitter. I found out later in life that my daughter's experiences with babysitters weren't always pleasant ones. Her quirky habit of smelling me — burying her head in my clothes to breathe in my fragrance — came from her need to keep me close. Breathing me in was her way of expressing her fear of abandonment, and her need to feel safe and protected. To this day, every time we hug, my daughter and I take deep, long breaths, and feel comforted and connected by the familiar smell of each other."

24 Security

"When I was a child my mother always did her best to make me feel cherished and safe. I still remember the sensation of being snuggled in a towelling beach robe after a cold swim in the sea or the importance of a favourite bedtime story at the end of a busy day at school. My mother still makes me feel calm and loved and I hope to give that to my own daughter as she grows up. It's a great foundation for life."

"When I was growing up my mother always said, 'Live for today and tomorrow will look after itself'. At that time, it helped me dismiss worries that I might have about scary events that were coming up – such as starting a new school. Now that I am a mum it reminds me to enjoy every moment that I have with my son and not to worry about the future, but to look forward to it."

I think what children need is love, security, stability, consistency and kindness.

Rosie O'Donnell

Wisdom

To know when to be generous and
when firm – that is wisdom.

Elbert Hubbard

My mother taught me that everyone I meet is as important as I am.

"My mother instilled in me 'Neither a borrower nor a lender be' – not to be beholden to anyone. I have found that it is better to give rather than lend. Lending destroys relationships."

"I learnt the value of listening from my mother. She always drummed it into us that we should never interrupt halfway through somebody's sentence. It was a worthwhile lesson – from really listening to people, I've gained far more insight into what they truly have to say."

"I learned so much from my mother: how to cook, how to become a lady. But mostly I learned that we are all here to help one another. My mother would do anything to help someone in need. She taught me that it was important to make the world a better place – that, in effect, we are our brothers' keepers. I treasure this as one of the most important lessons she taught me."

"My daughter and I bond on many levels, but often the roles have been reversed. I have 20 more years of life experience than her and believe myself to be an old soul, but there have been many times when my daughter seems even older. She came to me with an inner knowledge that only an experienced soul could possess. Even as a youngster, she helped me with the evolution of my own spirituality and, ultimately, the evolution of my true self."

33 Wisdom

Make your own fate: think positively and good things will happen.

"My relationship with my mother soured when I went to college. I rebelled and tried to prove my independence by resisting what she tried to teach me. After my career got going and I was on my own, I discovered that I liked a lot of things that my mother loves, such as working in the yard and cooking. During these awakenings I've learned that a lot of what she taught me was true. Even though our bond has been a half circle at times, we have come to have a good relationship and I love my mother. The more we mature, the more I appreciate her and ask questions, because I know there will come a day when no answers will be available, only history."

Tell me and I'll forget. Show me and I may not remember. Involve me and I'll understand.

Indian Proverb

"My mother's way of teaching me how to cook a meal was brutal but effective. She had to go into hospital for a minor op and arranged that I would cook my father's supper. I was 16 and had just left boarding school to become an apprentice journalist, so I knew nothing about cooking, except for the rock-hard rock buns taught in domestic science. She had bought a guinea fowl. Horrified, I asked how to cook same. 'I'm far too busy now – just as usual,' she said. So I consulted dozens of books and opted to cook the bird as if it were a chicken with added gratin dauphinois and a green salad (which I did know about). My father was delighted and I was triumphant. So much so that my mother was rather miffed. 'Well,' I asked, 'how would you have done it?' 'Don't ask me, darling, I've never cooked guinea fowl before either.'"

My mother always said 'Keep your eye on the doughnut, not the hole.' Concentrate on what you have, not what is missing.

'While we try to teach our children about life, our children teach us what life is all about.'

"My five year old loves listening to me tell stories about myself when I was her age. I enjoy telling them too, and find them to be extremely bonding because they help me remember how I felt, and how I saw the world at that young and innocent age. These stories put into perspective the things I expect from her, and she enjoys the feeling that we are in fact much closer than the 25 years between us."

"When my children became impatient with a task or a person, I would say to them, 'It's easier to catch flies with honey than it is with vinegar.' My mother told me the same thing, and it helped me to slow down and think carefully before speaking, rather than blurting something out."

Friends are very important. Look after your friends and they will look after you.

Strength

It takes courage to grow up and
become who you really are.

E. E. Cummings

"Finding an extra pinch of strength was a speciality of my mother's. As she said, if you can find something to laugh about, things can't be all bad. And there's always something to laugh about."

✳

"My mother taught me that — no matter how sad, scared or unwell I might feel — a good giggle works wonders. Even during the most challenging times, my mum is able to raise a laugh and make herself, and everyone around her, feel good."

"I lost my mother when I was 21. Today, even as an adult woman, I still think of her first when faced with a problem or when I need advice. I don't remember her doing or saying anything extraordinary to create our bond; she just always did whatever was in the best interest of her daughter. She kept it simple. Her words matched her actions. I felt safe and connected. Throughout my life, without any conscious thought, I selected other women to help me through rough times; situations that would ordinarily prompt a phone call to one's mother. I think I was so grounded in the bond I shared with my mother that I instinctively knew to whom she would want me to turn. Our bond lived on after her death and gave me the power to help myself. What a gift."

"When I was grieving over my separation from a boyfriend and agonizing over whether it could have worked out or not, my mother's remedy was to say, 'Oh love, write his name on a list and cross it off'. Sometimes you just have to accept that things are the way they are, but a little decisive action can help you feel more in control of the situation."

"Bonding with her daughters was a day-to-day affair for my mother. She loved to cook and always made sure we all ate together. She had us girls prepare the table and do the dishes. She taught us to do most of the household chores on our own. She was a disciplinarian, but a loving one. We witnessed her generosity, as well as her determination never to let anyone oppress our family or deprive us of our rights. She managed on her own to send us to school. I learned everything from my mum – especially how to be strong. She kept our family together."

"As a child, my mother allowed me to search, discover and find my way with support, love and understanding. She taught me to be open-minded and compassionate. She has been my voice of reason and my confidante through the years. I value her love and our friendship more than I can express and I am acutely aware that having a mother who is also one of my best girlfriends is one of the greatest gifts a daughter can be given."

Some good comes of everything, even
if you can't see what it is at the time.

"Once, when I was very depressed, at the age of about eight, my mother sat on my bed and said the reason I felt so bad was that I had 'an artistic temperament', which meant I was the kind of person who suffered extremes of emotion – sometimes I would feel very down but at other times I would feel ecstatically happy. This made being depressed seem an exotic advantage in life and instantly cheered me up."

*

"My mother taught me that giving up doesn't mean I'm weak. She always said that sometimes you have to be strong enough to let go. You don't know how much those words have rung true during my life."

*

"My mother gave me the courage to pursue my dreams, making me believe in myself and that I could achieve anything I put my mind to, as long as I worked hard enough."

If you're not where you want to be today,
keep putting one foot in front of the other and
you'll get there, one step at a time.

Legacy

Though we travel the world over to find the beautiful,
we must carry it with us or we find it not.

Ralph Waldo Emerson

"One of my mother's many qualities is her strong sense of justice and fairness. She has always been careful not to favour me over my younger brother, or vice versa, sometimes to an extreme degree. If I got some pocket money for sweets, he would get the same amount; if he got an ice cream on a trip with her, I would get the same when they returned home. I clearly remember the motto 'She who cuts doesn't choose', which was used on many occasions during my childhood. Needless to say, I developed a razor-sharp eye, which has meant that, from a very early age, I have been able to cut a cake in two pieces of exactly the same size. My mother's underlying sense of justice also taught me to remember that everyone deserves fairness – not only when it comes to cake – and that all people should be treated as equals."

"My mother advised 'Don't be envious of what others have, for you don't know how they got it.' Now that I am older, I am aware of the truth of this and am very grateful for the little that I do have."

"My mum has always advocated that you can only ever do your best. She would never get cross if we didn't get the marks we were expecting from exams, and was proud no matter what. That's always stayed with me; she's never made me feel like a failure."

"My daughter is truly amazing. And I am grateful, because I know that in some small way, I am a part of that."

"When my mother went away for her work as a sales rep, I stayed with my grandmother. I missed her very much at night and often I couldn't get to sleep. She told me that when I missed her I should look out of the window at the night sky and find the brightest star. She said that she would also look for it at my bedtime, and it would reassure both of us. The star would always be in the sky, even if she was on another continent. I still look up occasionally and remember how looking at the stars comforted me. Now I'm an adult, star-gazing still gives me a feeling of immense calm."

"When I was four or five, my mother took me by train to see the ballet Giselle. I remember it as if it were yesterday… sitting on the train, going to the theatre, watching the ballet with my mouth open, thinking there could never be anything more beautiful. My mom had a great sense of culture, which she passed down to me."

Don't have any regrets about the past,
only new plans for the future.

"I once confided in my grown daughter, that I feared I'd made mistakes as a very young mother, and hoped she didn't feel as though she'd had a bad deal in that department. She turned to me with a beautifully tender smile and said, 'Mum, you're absolutely perfect. You always did the best you could – I know that – and I love you, please don't worry.' It made my heart sing. I must have done something right to have a daughter who could respond so compassionately."

"My mother and I share a love of gardening. She taught me how to garden, and through her I have come to see how much pleasure there is to be had in watching things grow. I now get huge satisfaction from growing and eating my own fruit and vegetables."

"As a child, I was advised by my mother through a strange process of osmosis. Whatever the circumstances, she responded in a positive way. In my teenage years, any criticism on my part was met with the same response: 'You can find some good in everybody.' I came to understand that tolerance towards others makes life both easier and richer."

"My mother instilled a love of reading in me as she read me bedtime stories and, later on, gave me the books that she had loved as a child. I think of her when I read favourite books to my own children and when they enjoy the same stories that she and I enjoyed together. A book can still transport me from everyday problems."

"My mum has influenced me in lots of little ways – how to cook my favourite dinner, the funny little phrases she uses – but I know now that she imparted many of her values and skills to me without either of us realizing it."

"Now I am a mother myself I am trying to work out what makes my mother so good at the job. She has always had interests outside the home – work, friends, culture and long games of tennis – but managed to make her three children feel that they were the centre of her universe (without ever playing the martyr). Mothers need to be both a lively, independent role model for the grown-up world to come and an endlessly patient, nurturing and loving figure for the fleeting years of childhood. Looking back, I think she got it just right."

I would say, 'That's not fair,' and my
mother would say, 'But life isn't fair.'

Learn to
appreciate the
wisdom gained
by a lifetime of
experiences.

"No matter how complicated life got when I was growing up, we found a way through it, and my mother put me first every time. She always made it seem so easy. When I was a child we used to watch the Sunday afternoon movie together. I particularly loved the musicals, and one weekend she taught me how to dance. We had so much fun waltzing round the living room to The King and I, and even now the thought makes me smile."

A mother's happiness is like a beacon,
lighting up the future but reflected also on the
past in the guise of fond memories.

Honoré de Balzac

Picture & text credits

Ph = photographer
Page I The home of interior journalist and blogger
Jill Macnair in London. www.jillmacnair.com Ph: Rachel
Whiting. **Page 2** The home of Jeanette Lunde
Frydogdesign.blogspot.com Ph: Debi Treloar. **Page 3**
The family home of Iris of irideeen.blogspot.com Ph:
Catherine Gratwicke. **Page 4** The home of Anne Bjelke
hapelbloggen.blogspot.no. Ph: Catherine Gratwicke. **Page 5**
The family home of Lea Bawnager, Vayu Robins & Elliot
Bawnager-Robins, owner of affär (www.affaer.dk). Ph: Debi
Treloar. **Page 7** The home of Inger Lill Skagen in Norway.
www.kasparasregnbue.blogspot.com. Ph: Debi Treloar.
Page 8 David Austin Roses www.davidaustinroses.com. Ph:
Debi Treloar. **Page 9** The home of Vidar and Ingrid Aune
Westrum. www.fjeldborg.no www.13tretten.no Ph:
Debi Treloar. **Page 10** The home of Jeanette Lunde.
Frydogdesign.blogspot.com. Ph: Debi Treloar. **Page 11**
The home of Vidar and Ingrid Aune Westrum.
www.fjeldborg.no www.13tretten.no Ph: Debi Treloar
Page 12 Ph: Laura Forrester. **Page 13** Ph: Polly Wreford.
Page 15 www.sarah-janedownthelane.blogspot.com
Ph: Rachel Whiting. **Page 16** The home of Jane Schouten of
Blog.alltheluckintheworld.nl. Ph: Rachel Whiting. **Page 18**
The Linen Shed, boutique B&B near Whitstable, Kent, UK.
www.linenshed.com. Ph: Catherine Gratwicke. **Page 19**
The London home of Creative Ann Shore of Story. Ph:
Debi Treloar. **Page 20** Ph: Claire Richardson. **Page 21**
Niki Brantmark of My Scandinavian Home.
www.myscandinavian home.blogspot.com. Ph: Rachel
Whiting. **Page 22** The Linen Shed, boutique B&B near
Whitstable, Kent, UK www.linenshed.com. Ph: Catherine
Gratwicke. **Page 25** The home of Carol McKeown, owner
of Baby Ceylon. Ph: Debi Treloar. **Page 26** Nicky Grace
www.nickygrace.co.uk Vintage Fabric & Gorgeous Things
Ph: Catherine Gratwicke. **Page 28** The garden of Debbie
Johnson, owner of Powder Blue – Home & Garden in
Leicester. www.powder-blue.co.uk Ph: Debi Treloar.
Page 29 Ph: Claire Richardson. **Page 31** Arendal Keramik
www.arendal-ceramics.com Ph: Debi Treloar. **Page 32** Ilaria
Chiaratti www.idainteriorlifestyle.com Ph: Rachel Whiting.
Page 33 Ph: Catherine Gratwicke. **Page 35** The home of
Yvonne Eijkenduijn of www.yvestown.com in Belgium. Ph:
Catherine Gratwicke. **Page 36** Ph: Martin Brigdale.
Pages 39 & 40 www.myfriendshouse.wordpress.com
www.jillmacnair.com Ph: Rachel Whiting.
Page 41 The London home of Creative Ann Shore of
Story. Ph: Debi Treloar. **Page 42** Arendal Keramik
www.arendal-ceramics.com Ph: Debi Treloar. **Page 43** The
Linen Shed, boutique B&B near Whitstable, Kent, UK
www.linenshed.com Ph: Catherine Gratwicke. **Page 44**
The home of Maria Carr of www.dreamywhitesonline.com
Ph: Rachel Whiting. **Page 47** Niki Brantmark of My
Scandinavian Home. www.myscandinavian
home.blogspot.com Ph: Rachel Whiting. **Page 48** Ph: Debi
Treloar. **Page 50** Ph: Amy Neunsinger. **Page 51** Ph: Caroline
Arber/designed and made by Jane Cassini and Ann
Brownfield. **Page 53** Niki Jones www.niki-jones.co.uk Ph:
Debi Treloar. **Pages 54 & 55** www.selinalake.co.uk Ph: Debi
Treloar. **Page 57** The home of James and Maria Backhouse
in London Ph: Debi Treloar. **Page 58** Ph: Michelle Garrett.
Page 61 The home of Åshild Moen-Arnesen in Norway
www.prydelig.blogspot.com Ph: Catherine Gratwicke.
Page 62 The home in Glasgow of textile designer Fiona
Douglas of bluebellgray. www.bluebellgray.co.uk Ph: Debi
Treloar. **Page 63** Ph: Catherine Gratwicke.

All text copyright © Ryland Peters & Small with the
following exceptions © Cheryl Saban (and originally
published by Ryland Peters & Small in *All About My Mother*)
Pages 10, 13 (top), **14** (bottom), **20** (top), **23, 24, 30**
(bottom), **33, 31** (middle), **38** (top), **45** (top), **46, 55**
(bottom), **56** (middle), **59** (top).